# Sia Y. Chandler

# LUKE
## the Loving Dog

### Luke Finds His Numbers

Illustrated by: Kasalina Bastian

WORKBOOK PRESS LLC
187 E Warm Springs Rd,
Suite B285, Las Vegas, NV 89119, USA

Website:        https://workbookpress.com/
Hotline:        1-888-818-4856
Email: admin@workbookpress.com

Ordering Information:
Quantity sales. Special discounts are available on quantity purchases by corporations, associations, and others.
For details, contact the publisher at the address above.

ISBN-13:      978-1-954753-45-7 (Paperback Version)


REV. DATE: 28/03/2022

Luke looks high.

Luke looks low.

Looking for his numbers where-ever he goes.


Where is the number 1?

It is in the tree!


Luke rounds up the number,

And off he goes,

Where he will find the other numbers

Nobody knows!

Luke looks high.

Luke looks low.

Looking for his numbers where-ever he goes.


Where is the number 2?

It is in the bird's nest!


Luke rounds up the number,

And off he goes,

Where he will find the other numbers

Nobody knows!

Luke looks high.

Luke looks low.

Looking for his numbers where-ever he goes.

Where is the number 3?

It is behind the Strawberry bush!

Luke rounds up the number,

And off he goes,

Where he will find the other numbers

Nobody knows!

Luke looks high.

Luke looks low.

Looking for his numbers where-ever he goes.


Where is the number 4?

It is on top of the hill!


Luke rounds up the number,

And off he goes,

Where he will find the other numbers

Nobody knows!

Luke found some numbers

And he is happy you see.

Look at his tail wag.

He is happy as can be.

Look at his tail go.

But he can't stop now,

There are 6 more numbers

To be found!

Over the hill,

Around and down,

Luke knows there are more number

To be found!

Luke looks high.

Luke looks low.

Looking for his numbers where-ever he goes.


Where is the number 5?

It is playing with sticks!


Luke rounds up the number,

And off he goes,

Where he will find the other numbers

Nobody knows!

Luke looks high.

Luke looks low.

Looking for his numbers where-ever he goes.

Where is the number 6?

It is on the Lilly Pad!

Luke rounds up the number,

And off he goes,

Where he will find the other numbers

Nobody Knows!

Luke looks high.

Luke looks low.

Looking for his numbers where-ever he goes.


Where is the number 7?

It is inside the snack jar!


Luke rounds up the number,

And off he goes,

Where he will find the other numbers

Nobody knows!

Luke looks high.

Luke looks low.

Looking for his numbers where-ever he goes.


Where is the number 8?

It is pulling the rope!


Luke rounds up the number,

And off he goes,

Where he will find the other numbers

Nobody knows!

Luke looks high.

Luke looks low.

Looking for his numbers where-ever he goes.

Where is the number 9?

Taking a nap on the slipper!

Luke rounds up the number,

And off he goes,

Where he will find the other numbers

Nobody knows!

Luke looks high.

Luke looks low.

Looking for his numbers where-ever he goes.

Where is the number 10?

It is flying with the butterflies!

Luke rounds up the number,

And puts it with the rest!

He has them all.

No more and no less.

Luke looked high.

Luke looked low.

There is no need to look anymore.

Luke found all of his numbers

1 through 10

They all came back

And even brought some friends.

www.ingramcontent.com/pod-product-compliance
Lightning Source LLC
Chambersburg PA
CBHW040901120626
46551CB00001B/115